Transport Then and Now

Helena Ramsay

Illustrated by
Lynda Stevens

CONTENTS

Look at the two photographs on these pages.

This is a city in 1912. People who lived then used several kinds of transport. Some were very different to the ones we use now.

This is a city today. What differences can you see?

We are going to look at many forms of transport with three children from different times in this century: the 1900s, the 1930s and the 1990s.

For most people in the early 1900s, there were fewer ways of getting around than there are today. Horses and horse-drawn vehicles were used for some journeys, but people often walked.

I walk four miles to school each day.

Can you imagine walking eight miles (12.8 km) to and from school?

People usually lived close to their schools and where they worked, but they still walked much further than we do today.

Perhaps you travel by bus to school. These days, many of us make quite long journeys by bus, car or train each day.

7

A hundred years ago, people did not travel far from home as often as we do now. People made long journeys only on special occasions.

Long journeys were often made in trains like this one. Steam engines ran on coal, and they were smoky and noisy.

8

Railway stations were busy, exciting places.
These platforms are crowded with passengers
on their way to and from the seaside.

Can you see the coal piled up in the **tenders**
behind the engines?

Nowadays, trains are usually powered by **diesel** fuel or electricity. They are faster and cleaner than the old steam trains. This is the French TGV, the fastest passenger train in the world. It can travel at 300 kilometres per hour!

Why is the train pointed at the front?

High-speed trains are **streamlined**. The train's pointed nose helps it to cut through the air. The old steam engines, with their blunt noses, were slowed down by air resistance.

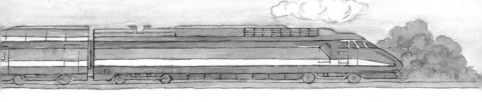

The trains of the future will travel even faster than the TGV. They will probably be maglev trains. These are trains that float along a few millimetres above the track. They are called maglevs because they are held up by **magnetic levitation**.

In some places, maglevs are already in use. This is a maglev train in Sydney, Australia.

When motor cars were first invented, they were expensive. Only very rich people could afford to buy them.

This 1907 Rolls Royce Silver Ghost was one of the most expensive cars ever built. Rolls Royce are still making expensive cars today.

By 1930, cars had become less expensive. Many more families were able to buy their own motor car. Gradually, cars became a convenient, everyday means of transport.

We go on outings to the country in our car.

Cars helped to change people's lives. It became easier to live out of town and travel to work in the city centre each day. This change affected the cities themselves. People moved out of the city centres to live in new homes in the **suburbs**.

Cars are still changing and developing today. The cars of the future will probably have electrically powered engines. Electric engines are clean and quiet. Unlike petrol engines, they do not create poisonous gases.

That car is a strange shape.

The body of this electric car can be detached from the **chassis**. The driver can then fit different bodies to suit different tasks.

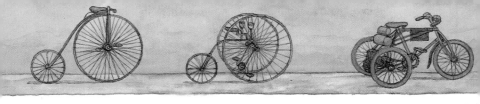

Bicycling has been a popular way to get
around since about 1885.

My father goes to
work on a bicycle.

Families often went bicycling in the country,
just as we do today. Their bicycles didn't look
very different to ours.

When cars became widely available, bicycles lost their appeal. Nowadays, many people are using bicycles again. They know that bicycles don't pollute the atmosphere, and that cycling helps to keep you fit.

The electric tram was introduced in about 1890. Trams ran on rails and were attached to overhead electric cables. The driver was called a motorman, and there was a conductor to help passengers and take their fares.

Most tram systems were closed down as more people used their own cars to travel to work.

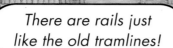

There are rails just like the old tramlines!

Today, electric trams have been re-introduced in some cities. This is because they cause less pollution than petrol-driven vehicles, and they help to reduce traffic jams in the city centres.

Until passenger aeroplanes were invented, the only way to cross the ocean was by ship.

I went to America by ship. It took us five days to get there.

The *Queen Mary* was one of the largest ships in the world. It could carry over two thousand passengers. Here you can see the *Queen Mary* arriving at New York City after her **maiden voyage** in 1936.

20

More than a thousand crew members worked
on each voyage to look after the passengers
and the ship.

For the richest passengers, the *Queen Mary*
was like a luxury hotel. There were several
dining rooms on board. The illuminated map in
this dining room showed the ship's progress
across the Atlantic Ocean.

Most passenger ships these days are ferries which are used for short journeys.

This passenger ferry is being pulled by a tugboat through the Corinth Canal, which is 6.5 kilometres long. If the canal hadn't been built, the ferry would have to travel 320 km round Southern Greece to get from the Aegean to the Adriatic Sea!

Nowadays, the biggest ships are used for the transportation of heavy **freight** around the world.

Look at the helicopter landing on that ship!

The largest form of transport ever built is the tanker. There are enormous supertankers that can carry half a million tonnes of crude oil in their holds.

In 1903, the Wright Brothers made the first powered flight in an aeroplane. This flight was the beginning of air travel.

This picture shows the first aeroplane to fly non-stop across the Atlantic Ocean, in 1919. It took sixteen hours and twenty-seven minutes, and the aeroplane made a crash landing in Ireland!

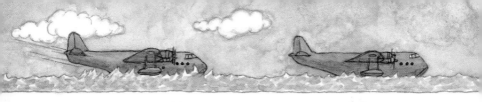

Flying boats, invented in the 1920s, were the earliest passenger aeroplanes. They were designed to land on large stretches of water, as there were few airports with runways.

It took 18 hours to fly the Atlantic!

Jet passenger services started at London Airport in 1952. This Comet aeroplane is about to make the first flight, to Johannesburg in South Africa.

Aeroplanes with jet engines are much faster than the old propeller-driven aeroplanes, but they use lots of fuel.

Concorde, the first **supersonic** jet airliner, began carrying passengers between London and New York in 1971.

Concorde looks like my paper dart!

Concorde's pointed shape helps to make it the fastest passenger aeroplane in the world. It travels at more than 2,000 kilometres per hour. That's twice the speed of sound! Crossing the Atlantic takes only three hours and fifty minutes.

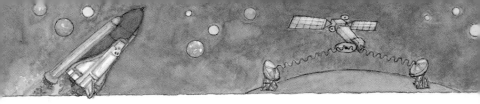

Nowadays we have forms of transport that were only dreamed of a hundred years ago.

This is a space shuttle right after blast-off. Rockets blast the shuttle into **orbit**. To escape the pull of **gravity**, a spacecraft must travel at a speed of forty thousand kilometres per hour!

It is even possible to travel in space without a vehicle. This astronaut is using a backpack which lets him move around without being attached to his spacecraft.

I think I'd like a backpack like that!

We have many new and exciting ways of travelling these days, but we have new problems, too. We need methods of transport that will not pollute the Earth's atmosphere or use up its scarce **resources**.

The forms of transport shown here have various sources of power. Do you know what they are? The answers are at the bottom of the page, but don't look until you have tried answering yourself.

1.

2.

3.

4.

5.

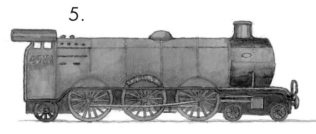

Answers: 1. Jet-propelled engine 2. Horse power 3. Pedal power 4. Electrically powered engine 5. Coal powered steam engine